CRACKING THE MOTOR MYSTERY

A Fun and Creative Approach to Gross Motor Basics

CATHY E. HARCKE, D.P.T.

ISBN-13: 978-1-4637-1162-7
ISBN-10: 1-4637-1162-X

DEDICATION

Cracking the Motor Mystery was written with a special thank you to all the little heroes who have taught and motivated me over the years. My patients and children inspired me to write this book. I have been amazed by their accomplishments and awed by their unbounded determination in their quest for fun, adventure, and achievement.

CONTENTS

ACKNOWLEDGMENTS

A special thank you is due to the friends and family members who shared their time, insight, and knowledge throughout the writing and editing process. You have all offered unique and valuable opinions to help make *Cracking the Motor Mystery* accessible to every reader. Thank you!

INTRODUCTION

Every child presents us with a unique challenge and mystery. Do you know a child who struggles with learning motor skills that others seem to learn without effort? Do you want your child to watch less television, but you are challenged with keeping your very active child entertained or motivating your more sedentary child to participate in physical activity? Are you searching for creative motor challenges for the children in your life? You can improve their strength, flexibility, motor coordination, and general fitness through play. You will decipher the code, and find a willing participant in gross motor activities, when you uncover what motivates each child.

I have a story to tell. The heroes in my story are the children who have touched my life. They were my teachers just as I was their teacher. They taught me what is fun and how to motivate them. I am a pediatric physical therapist as well as a mother. It is my job to motivate children to face challenges that are difficult and at times seem insurmountable. I believe in my little heroes. I have seen them attempt skills that many saw as unattainable and achieve great things. However, this book is not MY story. It is crafted to be a recipe for blending your child's interests with age appropriate motor skills to get your little hero off the couch and in motion. It is designed for parents, teachers, and therapists looking for creative methods to teach fundamental gross motor skills.

CHAPTER 1

GETTING STARTED

The essential ingredient in teaching anything, including motor skills, is motivation! Getting a child interested in participating is the most important component in teaching. I have many years of experience in pediatric physical therapy. However, even during my first year of working in pediatrics, parents would comment that their child was progressing quickly and greatly enjoying therapy sessions. The child was not responding to my doctorate degree, continuing education, or experience working with children. All of these things are important in attaining professional competence. However, the progress I saw came from the children wanting to do what I asked them to do, even if it was difficult for them, because I found a way to make a connection to what motivated or inspired each child. This book has many examples of how to transform something first perceived as difficult, boring, or even impossible into something fun and relatable.

The title of *Cracking the Motor Mystery* grew from this

concept of uncovering a child's true motor potential by combining creativity with knowledge to facilitate learning and practicing difficult skills. Creativity can completely alter a child's perspective of an activity and make a difference in how easily skills are acquired. A frustrated child will put more effort into learning a challenging skill if it involves an interesting game. I have seen this method work in my therapy sessions over the years. I consider it a professional accomplishment that most of my patients have not merely improved their functional abilities but also enjoyed coming to physical therapy. I believe that this enjoyment of the play activities blended with their exercise programs boosted their motivation and compliance so that their progress was accelerated. Most successful pediatric therapists have discovered this very important key to success.

Most children enjoy movement. Their desire for mobility is further augmented by their drive to learn and explore. However, more and more, children's playtime has been steered toward sedentary activities of television and computer games. Knowing how to tap into this innate enjoyment of physical activity is an important skill and a way to balance out this increase in screen time. Higher energy children also can benefit from the activities in this book, which provide constructive outlets to channel their energy. Having a variety of games to play while practicing motor skills fuels excitement and interest in these activities. I have seen and reviewed many books with information on age appropriate gross motor skills for babies. However, acquisition of fundamental gross motor skills, basic movements generated by the large muscles of the body, continues well beyond first steps.

Cracking the Motor Mystery provides creative techniques to introduce and practice fundamental gross motor skills for children with the skill level of one year to five years age equivalency. School age children continue to build upon and refine these fundamentals. Even professional athletes had to start somewhere! This book belongs on the shelf of all of the following:

- Parents and teachers who want to learn creative ways to promote muscle strength, flexibility, coordination, and endurance

- Parents and teachers of children having difficulty acquiring gross motor skills and needing guidance and motivation to learn these skills

- Therapists seeking creative treatment or home program ideas

I hope that you enjoy these experiences and encourage you to create your own games as well. I am confident that in addition to promoting mastery of gross motor skills and increased physical fitness, this book will provide an avenue for building memories of shared experiences that last beyond childhood.

BEFORE YOU BEGIN

Before attempting the activities discussed in this book, please note the following:

- It is recommended that both the child and the adult providing assistance use appropriate footwear. Well fitting tennis shoes are ideal. Bare feet also may be used for indoor activities. Open toe or heel shoes provide less stability and may cause tripping.

- No activity should be performed if it causes pain (to the adult or the child). A medical doctor should be consulted if pain results when attempting an activity.

- If you or the child have a preexisting medical condition or physical disability, check with a medical doctor before practicing the skills in this book.

- A parent or supervising adult should guard closely with new skills, especially where level changes are involved, such as jumping activities and stairs.

- Let the child guide you. Not all children develop at the same rate. These activities should be fun and not stressful. Encourage, but do not force, the child to participate.

- Every child develops on his or her own time line, and any ages listed in this book are meant to serve as guidelines. Since *Cracking the Motor Mystery* is relevant to children with and without motor delay, it does not focus on specific age recommendations, but instead on the activities and activity progression. If you have questions about more specific age expectations of certain skills, please consult your child's pediatrician.

- Since this information applies to both girls and boys, I alternate between use of female and male pronouns throughout the book.

POSSIBLE CONCERNS

Children develop at their own rate. There is not an exact timetable to develop gross motor skills, but there is an age range when you will likely see these skills emerge. For example, some children without orthopedic or neurologic impairments may walk as early as nine months and some not until eighteen months. However, there is at times a medical reason for gross motor delay, and the sooner it is addressed, the better the outcome may be. Parents should consult their pediatrician if they have any concerns about their child's development., especially if they have noticed significant developmental delay relative to other children the same age, excess stiffness of joints or tightness of muscles, involuntary movement (at rest or when attempting another movement), pain complaints during motor activities, unusual alignment or positioning of body parts, or strong side preferences that are not developmentally appropriate (such as limping when walking or avoiding using one hand).

ATTITUDE ALERT

As a clinician, you learn the fine line between pushing and encouraging. You also learn that every parent has a distinct comfort level with how much he is willing to stretch the boundaries of his child's comfort zone, and every child has a unique personality in regard to how he approaches challenges and new activities. A professional reads each patient as he gets to know that individual. A parent already knows his child well. The dare devil with no safety awareness cannot be approached the same way as the child who is afraid of trying new things. These activities are designed to be fun and to make children want to participate, not be forced into it. Tears and trips to the emergency room are not part of this recipe for success. Safety is always the first priority! Do not push a child to do skills that he is not ready to do, and always guard a child from falling while practicing new skills until you see that he has mastered them. Do not force a child to do something that he does not want to try. Instead, motivate him with something that he is excited about and interested in playing. A child may not want to hop on his weaker leg, but he may be willing to attempt it if the goal is to set up his favorite train table once he gets to the other side of the room. In fact, the exercise itself may become fun if a knowledgeable adult knows how to facilitate the activity so that the child is successful and not frustrated (for example, holding the child's right hand while the child hops on the left leg).

How do you get started? We start with what happens AFTER those first steps. Learning to walk is just the beginning of gross motor development.

CHAPTER 2

BEYOND FIRST STEPS

It happens gradually, but when you look back, it seems like an instant. After months of reading the week to week guide of motor development, at last you see your precious little one take her first steps. The video cameras come out, and everyone is excited by this major accomplishment. However, what happens after those first and second steps? The answer is a lot of excitement, but also a lot of bandages and bumps as your baby finds her way in the world on two feet. Learning to balance and negotiate her environment creates new challenges every day. Parents and other caregivers may wonder how to help and what comes next. Many children pass through this next phase of development quite naturally without any interference but benefit from learning novel, age appropriate gross motor challenges during playtime. Some children are more timid and passive in their explorations of their environment and benefit from assistance in attaining new skills. Some children have physical disabilities that impair their ability to move forward with these skills. All of these children can benefit from the following information. In the case of a child with a physical or neurological disability causing delay in motor skills, consultation with a physical therapist and/or occupational therapist may be necessary and should be discussed with her pediatrician. This chapter talks about what happens beyond walking and how to have fun with these new talents. Remember that the goal is to incorporate these fun activities into your everyday playtime and not see them as an extra thing that you need to do with your children. I am a mom too and understand busy schedules. In fact, I started writing this book while lying on the floor next to my baby's crib during a bad teething week, and she is now seven years old!

WALKING CHALLENGES AND OBSTACLE COURSES

Obstacle courses and climbing are most often practiced in a clinical setting or on a playground, but the skill set gained with these activities can be performed anywhere. New walkers lack balance. They may be quite stable on flat, even surfaces but have difficulty walking on inclines (up and down hills), soft and uneven surfaces (grass, soft mats, tanbark, sand, etc.), through narrow passageways (between furniture or other closely spaced objects), over obstacles (plenty in any home with a toddler), and up and down level changes (steps). You don't need an expensive clinical set-up to practice these skills. Gaining skill and confidence with these challenges will minimize the minor, and sometimes major, injuries that all toddlers get. Once a child is walking with good stability on flat, even surfaces, he may be ready to try some of these skills. Signs of good stability include walking with feet apart to about shoulder width as opposed to a wide base of support, letting his arms fall to his side as opposed to keeping them up and out to the side, and, of course, walking without falling. If you are not sure that the child is ready for the following challenges, offer additional support, such as holding one or both hands, until you are more confident in his ability.

Many parks have grassy, inclined areas to practice walking up and down hills. When first trying this activity, choose smaller inclines and stand in the direction that the child is likely to fall. If the child is walking uphill, there is a backward fall risk so you should stand behind and within reach of him. If he is walking downhill, he will be more likely to lose control by accelerating or falling forward. In this case, if the incline is not very steep, it is safest for the child if you are standing in front of, but facing, him. Your safety is important as well! If you are not comfortable in this backward position, or if the hill is too steep to safely navigate it while facing the child, stand next to him, with a hand on him if needed, anticipating a possible forward fall so you are ready to intervene if necessary. As with all skills and exercises discussed, toys and games can be incorporated into this activity. For example, you can bring a toy car or ball up the hill, roll it down the hill, and walk down to retrieve the toy. Practice opportunities are also throughout the community. For instance, walking up wheelchair/ stroller ramps is another opportunity to practice this skill.

Soft and uneven surfaces provide a balance challenge because they require good proprioceptive feedback to maintain stability. We are able to maintain our balance using proprioception (the ability to identify the relative position of our own body parts, including joint position), vision, and vestibular sense (inner ear mechanism to sense head position and movement). Soft surfaces demand more joint, especially ankle, movement and the body must maintain balance despite these constantly, but subtly, changing joint positions. This is the reason that a new walker is more likely to fall on grass or in sand than on a flat, hard surface. As luck would have it, practicing walking on soft surfaces provides the double benefit of advancing balance with gait and providing a safe, cushioned surface to fall on. Walking on soft surfaces, such as couch cushions or pillows on the floor, is a fun way to practice this exercise at home.

New walkers utilize a wide based gait to maximize stability. Therefore, they have difficulty narrowing their base of support (walking with their feet closer together) to negotiate a narrow passageway without turning sideways. This skill can be practiced by setting up a pathway between closely placed furniture or boxes. Stand at one end of the passageway and start the child at the other end. Entice him to walk forward through the narrowed path with any motivation that interests the child, such as popping bubbles or retrieving a favorite toy. This activity is actually a balance challenge since it requires using a narrower base of support. Narrow walkways around your home or community also offer opportunities to practice this skill.

Stepping over obstacles requires prolonging the single limb stance phase of walking as one foot steps over the obstacle. At first, it is a difficult balance challenge. The goal is to challenge the child without tripping him. Start with an almost flat obstacle on the ground, such as a hula hoop to step over into the center, when first introducing this activity. The safety advantage of mastering this skill is obvious, including less tripping over toys and more stability when negotiating playground surfaces. Always guard the child closely to steady or catch him to avoid falls.

Walking up and down a single step or level change poses a challenge as well as a fall risk. You are able to most effectively guard the child from falling down the step if you are in front of the child and facing him when he steps down and behind the child when he steps up. Similar to stepping over an obstacle, stepping up or down a step requires a prolonged amount of time on one foot compared to walking. In addition, a child cannot successfully ascend a step without adequate quadriceps strength to lift his body weight to the next level. Stepping down presents the additional challenge of requiring the quadriceps to work eccentrically, in a lengthened and less advantageous position. Therefore, you may see children turning to the side to gain support from the collateral ligaments of the knee when first attempting level changes.

You can design an obstacle course in your living room and include some of the above skills in sequence. For example, you may line up a narrow passageway between two boxes or pieces of furniture, couch cushions to practice stepping up/ down and walking on soft surfaces, an inflatable or foam swimming pool toy or a hula hoop to step or climb over, and a tunnel (blanket draped over two pieces of furniture) to crawl through. You may need to provide support by holding one or two hands as needed during some of these challenges until the child can safely complete the activities without help.

BACKWARD WALKING

Backward walking is a skill that toddlers begin to do for

practical reasons, such as backing up when opening a door. Often, you will see toddlers walking backward across a room because it is a fun, new skill. They use this skill to pull toys as well. In fact, introducing pull toys with strings, as opposed to firm handles, is an excellent way to encourage learning this skill. If you pull a toy by the string while forward walking, you cannot see the toy because it drags behind you. Backward walking allows the child to view the toy and make it go at the same time. Children typically step with one foot to the place even with the other foot with early backward walking, progressing to using a normal stride length.

In order to walk backward, you need to weight shift briefly from one foot to the other, similar to forward walking. However, backward walking requires hip extension of the leg in swing motion (moving the hip of the leg taking the step backward), versus flexion (moving the leg forward at the hip), and the trunk strength to slow backward momentum. Otherwise, a loss of balance and fall would occur. It is important that the child walks safely and easily forward and has backward protective extension (reaction to place hands down if a backward fall occurs) before working on this skill without close guarding and/or assistance.

Older children with motor delay may be cognitively beyond being excited by pull toys. Backward walking still can be incorporated with play and more age appropriate challenges. They can choreograph a dance with the supervising adult that involves backward steps. They can pretend to be trucks backing up on a road or gymnasts where a taped line on the floor is the pretend balance beam. Backward walking also can be incorporated easily into many of the motor games described in chapter four. The possibilities are endless and are limited only by each child's interests.

SIDESTEPPING

Sidestepping requires strength and coordination. It involves shifting weight between the right and left leg and coordinating the use of several muscles in the correct sequence. When taking a step to the side, the hip abductors move one leg to the side and then help stabilize the hip as the adductors bring the other leg back in line with the body. Hip abductors are muscles usually on the outside (lateral side) or back (posterior side) of the hip that move the thigh outward away from the body. Hip adductors are muscles mostly on the inside (medial side) of the hip that move the thigh inward toward the body. Building skill with sidestepping also helps with balance and is an important precursor to other gross motor activities.

Fun ways to use and practice sidestepping include walking in a circle while holding hands and singing a favorite song, dancing to music with side steps, and walking sideways on a line, board, or curb. If practicing with a toddler, turn on the child's favorite music and hold hands while facing the child. Dance by stepping sideways to the right and then switch directions to the left after a few steps. As balance improves, attempt your dance while holding only one hand. When the child is ready, progress to activities without holding hands, such as walking sideways on a tape or chalk line. Activities are selected according to the child's interests, which determine what toy or game is at the other end of the line. This is a good opportunity to illustrate the countless play options that one has with a single motor skill. While practicing walking sideways, forward, or backward on a line with my patients, I have played all of the following activities:

- Walking across a bridge to attend a tea party

- Placing puzzle pieces with the pieces at one end of the line and the board at the other

- Engaging in a play pirate sword fight after crossing the bridge

- Rescuing people or pets from a pretend fire after carrying a foam cylinder "hose" across the bridge

- Activating a simple light-up switch toy

- Placing rings on a ring stacker

- Placing people or farm animals in a house or barn play set

- Pretending to be an Olympic gymnast

- Building a pretend meal, such as a pizza (one slice at a time) or a sandwich, with play food

- Crossing a bridge to find treasure (gold star stickers)

- Taking a turn or two at a board game after each time across the line

- Building a train track, one or two pieces at a time, with the pieces at one end of the line and train table at the other

- Building block towers, houses, or formations

- Dressing a doll at one end of the line by carrying the clothes, one item at a time, from the other end of the line

- Picking one card after each time across the line while playing a card game

As you can see, the options are never-ending and can include anything that the child likes to do. The list above easily could extend to one hundred games and includes activities to do with children ages one to ten, all practicing the motor challenge of sidestepping. These ideas are revisited in chapter four when balance beam and line walking is discussed. I hope that you can apply this creativity to find the perfect motivation for the children in your life and use this technique as we move on to other motor skills.

RUNNING

There is an expression that you have to walk before you can run. It is, for the most part, true. Running requires a bilateral swing phase of the gait cycle. For non-therapists, this means that true running involves an instance of both feet off the ground at the same time. Toddlers typically first "run" by walking quickly. Running games of chase and tag are great fun and best performed in large open spaces on safe surfaces, such as grass. This is one skill when you can truly see personality differences emerge. No one ever had to encourage my children to run, and they often pushed their limits on this skill before their bodies were ready. We had an enormous bandage supply in the medicine cabinet for this reason. However, from a clinical perspective, I have worked with many children who needed a little encouragement and motivation to take off with this skill. The advantage of tag is that there is a goal of speed to be achieved. If playing with siblings, I prefer to have the older sibling be the target, not the chaser, so that the child developing the skill has a goal of speed (to catch their sibling) and the older, larger sibling doesn't bulldoze the younger, slower child. This activity may require you to request the cooperation of the older sibling to eventually get caught and avoid frustrating the younger child. You can also set up small, but toddler safe, animals or people to place in play sets across the room after running back and forth to retrieve them. Racing to collect pieces to simple puzzles and shape sorters can work well for running games as well.

For older toddlers and preschoolers attempting to learn this skill or practice running, games of make-believe are helpful. You can play fire fighters who have to rescue people or stuffed animals on one side of the room or yard and run back to the other side as quickly as you can. You can also do a tower building contest by placing the blocks on one side of the play area and building on the other side. The game becomes a race of who can collect their blocks first with the bonus of building the tower after running back and forth to retrieve the blocks. The same game can be played with puzzles by placing the pieces on one side of the room and the puzzle frames on the other side. For outdoor play, ball games can be used to encourage running. For example, you can kick a ball a desired distance and have the child run to throw or kick it back to you. As you can see by the list already generated, the possibilities are endless and can be tailored to the interests and age of the child.

TIPTOE STANDING AND WALKING

Tiptoe standing and walking are important precursors to

other skills. Tiptoe standing requires the balance to stand on a smaller base of support versus standing on the entire surface of your feet. In addition, a significant amount of muscle strength is required. Your calf muscles, including your gastrocnemius and soleus muscles, are contracting to achieve tiptoe standing. However, other muscles, such as hip extensors and abdominals, must work in conjunction with this group in order to maintain upright posture in this position. The strength gained with this skill helps children later progress in other gross motor skills that require lower extremity power, such as jumping and hopping.

It is simple to entice a child to attempt tiptoe standing. You can hold an object of interest slightly out of reach. This object may be a toy, cup, sticker, or bubble caught on a wand when blowing bubbles. It is important that you avoid teasing and allow the child to obtain the object when she rises to tiptoes. Activities that allow for repeated heel raises work best, such as placing stickers or magnets, collecting puzzle pieces to do a puzzle, or popping bubbles. Tiptoe standing can be initiated by first attempting the skill with upper extremity support so that maintaining balance is not required. An example is reaching for magnet letters that are slightly out of reach on the refrigerator. The child is able to lean forward against the refrigerator for support while reaching with the other hand and rising to tiptoes. Over time, this activity is progressed to reaching for items without having upper extremity support so the child is challenged with simultaneously maintaining balance and generating muscle power.

Once tiptoe standing without support is achieved, tiptoe walking can be attempted. Encourage the child to straighten her knees and keep her heels off the ground as you demonstrate the exercise. With practice, the child will be able to increase the number of steps and overall distance. Toe walking can be incorporated into a variety of games, as described in chapter four, or used as a fun imitation activity.

BALANCE ACTIVITIES WITH SINGLE LIMB STANCE

One foot balance is required for many gross motor activities. Even walking has a period of single limb stance while the other leg swings forward to take a step. The ability to support weight on one foot is also required for running, marching, hopping, skipping, galloping, walking over obstacles, kicking, and climbing up and down stairs. Some of these skills will be discussed in later sections, but there are many beginning balance activities that allow for practice in brief single limb stance. Marching is a great way to initiate the ability to maintain balance on one foot because it demands only brief periods of single limb stance, just a slightly prolonged one foot standing phase versus with walking. You can even have a parade with play instruments. Stomping, like marching, involves an extended single limb balance time on the weight-bearing leg, and it can be practiced by popping bubbles on the floor or during a dance activity. Kicking requires brief one foot standing on the supporting leg. Initially, kicking can be practiced with stationary objects that won't roll away from the child, such as toy bowling pins, cardboard blocks, or empty milk or juice cartons that have been washed out. Stepping over low obstacles results in brief single limb stance on the leg left behind when initiating the step and then on the front leg as the other leg is brought forward. Games may include stepping over a threshold to enter a playhouse or stepping over a hula hoop to get to a toy in the center. Since all of the activities discussed in this section require a phase of one foot standing, they can all be considered beginning balance activities.

RIDING CARS

Toddler riding toys, cars or other vehicles that the child propels with his feet while sitting, are great precursors to riding a tricycle. These toys provide surprisingly great exercise by requiring use of lower extremity muscles, including hamstrings, quadriceps, and calf muscles. You may see children pushing their knees into extension and successfully achieving backward before forward movement. You can encourage practice riding in both directions, but be aware that toddlers do not always notice obstacles in their path, especially if pushing backward. Like all activities with this age group, playtime should be closely supervised. Forward riding requires more skill in motor planning to sequence muscle action and lower extremity position. It is also more functional in using the toy as a vehicle to move from place to place and better allows for changing directions as right and left lower extremity dissociation is learned (right and left legs alternating movement and not moving simultaneously to mirror each other).

REVIEW OF ACTIVITIES

Many activities were introduced throughout this chapter while discussing motor skills. These activities included the following:

- Walking up and down inclines/ climbing up to race cars or roll a ball and climbing down to retrieve it

- Walking on couch cushions or pillows placed on the floor

- Walking through a narrow passageway to retrieve a toy of interest or pop a bubble

- Stepping over a low obstacle to find a toy of interest

- Walking up and down a single step or level change

- Walking backward while pulling a pull toy with a string

- Sidestepping to dance in a line or circle while singing a fun song or listening to music

- Sidestepping on a line with countless play options

- Running games of tag

- Racing back and forth to play rescue, construct a tower, complete a puzzle, or chase and return a kicked ball

- Tiptoe reaching for magnets on the refrigerator, small toys, bubbles caught on the wand, puzzle pieces, stickers, etc.

- Tiptoe walking

- Marching in a parade with play instruments

- Stomping to pop bubbles on the floor or perform a dance activity

- Kicking a stationary object and progressing to kicking a ball

- Riding on a toddler vehicle that is propelled by the child's feet

The above skills are excellent to practice with a child with the motor age equivalency of a toddler. A few games for older children were mentioned in discussion of these activities to give options for children with motor delay who are still learning these skills. Several months of gross motor practice after first learning to walk may be needed to acquire the necessary balance and strength to participate in some of these challenges. Jumping and stair climbing often begin to emerge in the toddler age group as well. However, these skills are discussed in the next chapter because they typically become mastered in the preschool age group. The following chapter addresses how to facilitate acquisition of fundamental gross motor skills for older toddlers, preschoolers, and school age children still learning gross motor basics.

CHAPTER 3

TEACHING FUNDAMENTAL SKILLS

I have included this chapter to assist with problem solving how to teach and progress certain fundamental gross motor skills most effectively. We all know some children who acquire these skills with ease. My niece was hopping across the living room, without putting her foot down between hops, before turning three years old (more typically a three to five year-old skill). However, many children could benefit from some knowledgeable assistance to make acquiring these skills less frustrating. As a bonus, the process of working on these skills together can be fun. These techniques can be used for children with and without motor delay. They can be effectively utilized when participating in the activities described in the next chapter, "Fun Activities for Practice and Play," if the child requires assistance. You may want to refer back to this chapter if the child has difficulty learning the gross motor skills that serve as the foundation of the games in chapter four. Suggestions for helping with other skills that are not mentioned here are detailed in the subsequent chapter during discussion of each activity. This chapter gets you started with teaching some important gross motor basics.

CLIMBING STAIRS

A supervising adult should always be present when practicing the following stair skills. Stair practice can be dangerous because there is a fall risk. It is better to ere on the side of caution and to begin with providing additional support for safety. You can reduce your support as the child proves his stability, but remain ready to assist and within reach. Some homes have stairs, and children in these environments may learn these skills earlier because of the opportunity to practice. Most play structures at parks and many buildings throughout your community have stairs. Therefore, stair climbing and safety is one of the most functional gross motor skills that a child learns. He will encounter them throughout childhood so it is best to practice to gain coordination, strength, and balance with this activity while an adult is readily available to assist. As with any skill or activity, safety is the first concern. The following discussion will help you understand how to help children learn these skills. The next chapter will give you ideas of how to bring fun to this very important functional skill.

Ascending Stairs

Children are motivated to climb. Typically, children

learn to crawl up stairs before they begin walking up. When first walking up steps, a child usually places both feet on each step instead of alternating feet. You can begin by holding both hands or holding one hand and having her hold a rail with the other hand so that bilateral support is provided. As her skill improves over time, you can reduce your assistance to unilateral support (holding the railing OR holding one hand). Eventually, she will begin to alternate feet so only one foot is on each step when she has support but continue to place both feet on each step if walking up without support of a railing or hand-hold. Ultimately, when the child has adequate strength, balance, coordination, and leg length, you will see her climbing up by alternating feet with her hands free or while holding a toy. If the child has the confidence and stability to walk up a flight of stairs with her arms relaxed at her side, instead of held up and out to the side in an effort to gain postural stability, she may be able to safely carry a toy with both hands. Start by offering a soft toy or ball so that she is not injured if she falls forward on the toy. Remember that safety is especially important with stair climbing. You should always be standing behind the child when she walks up stairs. This position allows you to guard against a potential fall backward and help steady the child if she starts to fall forward. It is important to guard closely until she consistently has proven her stability at each level of assistance.

Descending Stairs

Descending stairs follows a progression similar to ascending stairs. Children usually begin to descend stairs by scooting down while seated or by crawling down backward (feet first). When a child first attempts walking down stairs, he usually requires bilateral hand support with both hands held or one hand held and the other on a railing. As you notice the child gaining stability and strength, you can reduce the level of assistance to unilateral support so that you are only holding one hand or the child is holding the railing without help. If you are not providing hands-on assistance, it is best to stand in front of, facing, and within reach of the child so that you are able to catch him if he begins to fall down the stairs. You should only attempt this backward or sideways position if you have access to a railing for support, are comfortable in this position, and have no balance or orthopedic impairments that would compromise your safety and that of the child. When he first begins to walk down steps without upper extremity support, he most likely will use a step-to pattern with both feet on each step instead of alternating with only one foot placed on each step. However, he may choose to alternate feet if holding a railing but place both feet on each step if carrying an object. Ultimately, stairs are negotiated reciprocally with one foot on each step without support of a hand-hold or railing.

Likely Progression of Ascending/Descending Stairs:

1. Both hands held
2. One hand held and one on railing
3. One hand held/ other hand free
4. One hand on railing/ other hand free
5. Hands free

Each of these phases may show progression from both

feet on each step to alternating feet so one foot is on each step. If the child is still placing both feet on each step, notice if he consistently uses the same leg to initiate the step up or down. If so, you can encourage him to "take a turn with the other leg" sometimes. When ascending stairs, greater muscle demand is placed on the leg initiating the step up. Skill is usually achieved first with ascending steps. Descending stairs requires eccentric, versus concentric, quadriceps control. The muscles are required to work in a less advantageous lengthened position with eccentric muscle use. When stepping down, greater muscle demand is placed on the leg left behind, not the leg initiating the step down. A child who lacks adequate quadriceps strength, or who is new to practicing this skill, may attempt to turn to the side to go up and down steps. This position allows the collateral ligaments of the knee to provide passive structural control, versus relying on muscle strength and activity. Encourage the child to face forward, not sideways, with stair climbing. The strength gained with this practice is essential for the development of many other gross motor skills, such as jumping.

JUMPING

Jumping is a fundamental skill often acquired beginning at age two. Children typically learn to jump up, jump forward, and jump down from a surface. Initially, jumping involves a one-foot take off and landing (feet not moving at the same time so one foot takes off from the ground and lands before the other) but progresses to jumping with two feet moving simultaneously. When you see this skill emerging, you can attempt to hold hands to gently assist with balance and the lift of the jump. As the child becomes more independent with jumping, you can progress to offering just one hand to assist. It is important that you do not pull up on the child's arm against the shoulder joint to pull her off the ground, but instead help her with the lift that she has already initiated on her own.

Once the child is able to jump up and land with her feet moving simultaneously, you can encourage her to attempt forward jumping. Begin by holding two hands or one hand if needed, gradually increasing the distance of the jump and decreasing the amount of assistance provided. Safety is your first concern. Do not perform this activity on an unsafe surface or pull the child's arms. Just offer support and balance. Visual cues are most helpful and motivating to encourage achieving greater distances. For example, you can arrange cut pieces of a no-adhesive shelf liner in a line on the floor to create a slip resistant surface for jumping from one "lily pad" to another. Distance is set by the ability of the child. You can also use these visual markers to increase the number of times jumped consecutively (further description in the next chapter), with the goal of maintaining two feet together and not taking steps between jumps. A jump rope placed flat on the ground can serve as a pretend sleeping snake, a visual cue to gain greater distance with jumping forward and over it.

Jumping down from a low surface requires a small jump forward and a little courage. Toes should begin at the edge of the step to avoid tripping. Gravity provides assistance once the forward jump in the air is achieved. As with jumping up and forward, difficulty of this activity can be increased by reducing the support provided from holding both hands, to holding one hand, to guarding closely without providing physical assistance.

Jumping over obstacles is a more advanced skill and should be attempted only with close guarding by a responsible adult to prevent a possible fall. Also, a gradual progression of obstacle height should be considered. Follow the cues of the child with what she attempts, but keep in mind that preschoolers do not always exhibit good safety awareness.

HOPPING

Hopping is simply a jump on one foot. Consequently, it requires both adequate strength to push your body weight off the ground and the balance to stand on only one foot when pushing off and landing. Both jumping and one foot standing are excellent skills to practice if the child is having trouble learning to hop. In addition, any exercises that improve balance and promote lower extremity strengthening, especially of the quadriceps (anterior thigh), gastrocnemius (superficial calf), and soleus (deeper calf) muscles, are helpful. These skills include climbing stairs, riding a tricycle, tiptoe standing or walking, jumping games, single limb stance activities, and balance beam or line walking. Activities with heel raises, discussed in chapter two, can be progressed to single limb heel raises while the child holds your hand or a stable support surface, as needed for balance. If the child knows how to jump and is attempting to hop, he may learn more quickly and experience less frustration if you provide some assistance. To begin with, you can hold two hands, progressing to one hand, as with jumping instruction. When holding one hand, you provide more support when holding the hand opposite the leg that is hopping. In other words, hold the child's right hand if he is hopping on the left foot with the right foot off the ground. Do not pull on the child's arm to lift him with force. You are simply providing balance assistance. Similar to jumping, it is easier to hop in place (landing in the same place that you start from) compared with achieving forward movement with hopping. Consecutive hopping, hopping a number of times in a row without putting the other foot down between hops, adds a level of difficulty, especially if combined with forward movement across the room. Challenge the child according to his ability level. Hopping often begins to emerge at age three with skill progression continuing at age four to five. However, the suggested exercises and progression of skill are not age dependent and should be utilized when the child is developmentally ready.

SKIPPING

The key to learning skipping is to break the skill down into parts. Skipping is a series of steps and hops, alternating between sides (left step, left hop, right step, right hop, left step, etc.). For some children, it is easier to learn this pattern if they practice slowly in this step-by-step way. You can also provide assistance with the hopping portion of the skill by holding one hand. Other children acquire this skill naturally or by watching others. Once a child establishes a smooth rhythm with skipping, she will bring her leg forward in preparation for the next step while it is already lifted to hop on the opposite foot. By performing these motions simultaneously, she gains efficiency and speed.

Galloping is a good precursor to skipping because it practices transferring weight between legs and does not require the coordination of sequencing the switch between right and left sides. Once mastered, skipping is an excellent endurance exercise. It can be used during a variety of games as a way to get from one place to another, such as during the toy hunt game described in the next chapter. Skipping often emerges in four to five year-olds but may be seen before or after this age. Throughout this book, keep in mind that there is a range of "normal," and every child develops at his own rate. Also, children with gross motor delay often acquire these fundamental skills eventually, but they achieve these milestones on their own time lines.

If you are feeling overwhelmed with detailed technical descriptions, there is no need for concern. Not every child requires help with every skill. Please refer back to this chapter if you are having trouble helping with an activity in the next chapter. If you have read this far, you have earned some fun!

CHAPTER 4

FUN ACTIVITIES FOR PRACTICE AND PLAY

Now that you know how to help and encourage children learning fundamental gross motor skills, you can let your creative side blossom and the child in you emerge. It is time to have fun with all the basics!

TREASURE HUNT

Treasure hunt is my favorite game to play during therapy sessions. This game involves hiding objects of interest and using different gross motor skills as the child seeks the hidden objects. At Easter time, I often do egg hunts with my patients. I like to hide gold star stickers as buried treasure and play pirates seeking treasure. You can hide play food pieces and create a pretend meal after collecting them. Here is the catch. The instructions sound something like,

"The treasure map says that you must skip twenty times toward the door to find the next piece." The next clue might read, "Hop toward the ball bin and hunt in that area until you find the next piece." You can also play "hot and cold" where the child is told they are "hot" when near a hidden object or "cold" when far away. The key is to work on any of the basics that we already discussed, including galloping, skipping, jumping, hopping, walking, running, sidestepping, marching, backward walking, etc. so that a motor challenge is occurring simultaneously with an enjoyable game.

ANIMAL WALKING

This activity can be played in the context of a "Simon Says…" game or just by itself for fun. Any animal can be used. Imitating animal movements requires strength and a good deal of motor planning and imitation skill to decipher how to create the desired movement. Motor planning is the ability to plan the correct sequence of movements in order to execute a skill, activity, or more complex movement. The following animal imitation activities can be easily used to create interesting and challenging motions:

- Bear Walking- The child walks on hands and feet with elbows and knees in near extension (straight arms and legs).

- Crab Walking- The child walks on hands and feet with his stomach facing the ceiling. Knees are bent, elbows are nearly straight and his bottom is off the ground. Some people refer to this alignment as a "table top" position where the chest and abdomen form the table and the legs and arms are the table legs.

- Snake Crawling- The child lies in prone (on his stomach) on the ground and moves by wiggling forward (alternating laterally flexing and extending the right and left sides of the body).

- Frog Hopping- The child squats with hands touching the ground and springs up and forward while partially extending knees and then landing in the starting position again.

- Any other favorite animal can be imitated as well. For example, a dog walk can be crawling in quadruped (hands and knees), or a penguin walk can be walking on heels, maintaining toes up. Be creative!

WHEELBARROW OR HAND WALKING

Wheelbarrow walking (hand walking) is an exercise where one person (the child) walks on her hands while another person (an adult) holds the child's legs. If you have orthopedic problems, such as knee or back pain, it is not recommended that you help with this activity. Hand walking is a favorite of my own children (age four and seven). Begin with the child on her hands and knees. Provide good trunk support as you lift her legs and she supports weight on her hands. If her arms collapse, you are holding her trunk so she will not fall. Ask her to put her hands down for support if she is not already in this position. You are kneeling behind the child with one of her legs tucked between your left arm and the left side of your body and the other leg tucked between your right arm and right side of your body. The amount of support that you provide at this point depends on the child's strength, particularly of the shoulder girdle and abdominals. Her back alignment should be relatively flat and straight, not raised like an angry cat or sagging toward the floor. If you see her unable to maintain this position and her back is sagging with her stomach toward the floor, ask her to make her back straight and correct the position. If she cannot correct her alignment, and you feel that she understands your instructions, she is not receiving enough support from you. I like to start with my hands at the child's hips. You can always move your hands down to the thighs if it is too easy for her, but if she cannot maintain a straight back in this position, move your hands back up to the hips. The farther from the hips toward the knees that you hold, the greater the difficulty, so place your hands as low on her legs as you can without her losing good, straight back alignment. It is recommended to keep your hand support above the knees. This position is usually sufficiently challenging for the preschool age group and will minimize stress to her knees and back. The adult helping is kneeling or squatting, instead of standing, to avoid stress to his own back, but do not walk on your knees if it causes pain or if you have a history of knee problems. Most adults standing in a fully upright position will pull the child out of optimal alignment. Also, check that the child's hands are flat with weight-bearing on her palms, not on her fists or finger tips, before you ask her to hand walk forward. Attempt to increase the distance, but allow for rest when you notice fatigue and loss of good alignment.

Often, it feels fun and silly to do just hand walking, but this activity can be made even more enjoyable while increasing the difficulty at the same time. Set up a line of empty juice or milk cartons (washed out first), lightweight blocks, or plastic bowling pins to knock over. Have the child do wheelbarrow walking along this line and knock over each obstacle as she comes to it. Ask her to take turns knocking over objects with the right and left hand.

"HOW MANY...TO MY FAVORITE STORE?"

In this game, one person, usually the adult to start, is the director of the game. The other participants are trying to tag him. First, the director stands at the end of the room or field opposite the other participants and calls out the activity to be performed. He may say, "Now we are skipping" or "Now we are jumping." This game works well when practicing walking, running, skipping, jumping, galloping, hopping, crab walking, bear walking, toe walking, heel walking, sidestepping, marching, or most other activities involved in locomotion. The children ask, "How many jumps (or skips, hops, etc.) to my favorite store (may fill in a name of a favorite store)?" The director replies, "five jumps," and all participants take five large jumps forward. The question is then repeated with a new number as the reply. Play continues until the director is tagged. If more than one child is playing, the person to reach the director first becomes the director and chooses the new motor skill to be performed. Although this game is fun on its own, a reward system can also be added if it helps to motivate a more hesitant child. For example, you can play

"How Many… to My Favorite Sticker Store?" and earn one sticker each time the director is reached. Another example is "…My Favorite Restaurant?" where the child earns play food items each round to create a pretend meal. Children are all unique and motivated by different rewards. Some other reward ideas that may encourage participation are listed as follows:

- "…My Favorite Art Store?" where the child acquires paint or markers to create a picture after tagging the director

- "…My Favorite Toy Store?" where the child earns a certain number of puzzle pieces, train track pieces, or blocks each round for assembling and building

- "…My Favorite Pet Store?" where the child selects an animal to "buy" and for the director to imitate (sound or action)

- "…My Favorite Bookstore (or Library)?" where the child either reads a short book at the end of the round or says the name of a book to be read later

- "…My Favorite Zoo?" where the child chooses an animal for the director to imitate (sound, action, or locomotion)

It is not recommended that food be used as a reward in this game since it may pose a choking risk to eat and participate in gross motor activities simultaneously.

STOP AND GO

In a manner similar to the previous game, one person acts as a director, or leader, and stands at one side of the play area. The remaining participants stand on the opposite side and face the director. The director says "go" or "stop" while the participants move forward with the chosen motor activity, as quickly as they can, in attempt to tag the adult or leader. If the adult says, "Go!" then the children jump (or some other declared motor activity such as skipping, hopping, galloping, marching, etc.) forward until the adult says, "Stop!" The first child to reach the director earns a reward or a turn to be the leader of the game for the next round. If someone is caught moving after "stop" has been called, she has to go back to the starting location. This game can be played with either two players (a director and participant) or many children, which makes it ideal for either a therapy session or a classroom activity. Play at home can include an adult and one child or many siblings.

STAIR FUN AND SAFETY

Mastering safety with stairs is very important in our environment, especially if your home has stairs. Clinically, stair skill is essential because it is such an important functional goal to safely access play structures and buildings in the community. If you have stairs in your home and your child is already interested in stairs, practice can merely involve walking up and down together, with your level of assistance depending on the child's skill level and safety awareness. If attempting to motivate a more hesitant child, employing a little creativity can be useful to create an interest in the activity. For instance, if your child likes puzzles, you can set up a puzzle board at the top of the stairs and place the pieces at the bottom of the stairs. Practice occurs as you walk down and up to retrieve the pieces and place them in the puzzle. The same activity can be performed with placing animals in a toy barn or building a sandwich with play food. The key is to create an activity that requires ascending and descending the stairs to complete the activity. A progression of this activity may look as follows.

Brian (fictional character) is a three year-old with stairs in his home. He lacks safety and consistency on the stairs. Brian's mother sets up a farm at the top of the stairs and six farm animals at the bottom of the stairs. At first, practice occurs with Brian and his mom each holding an animal and bringing them upstairs. Brian steps on one step at a time (both feet on one step) while holding his mom's hand. As the weeks progress, he gains independence and stability on the stairs. Next, Brian is able to go up the stairs in this same nonreciprocal pattern of both feet on one step without holding his mom's hand so he is able to hold an animal in each hand. If he is always stepping up with the same foot first, his mother may encourage him to take a turn with the other foot intermittently. At this phase, he is beginning to alternate feet, so that only one foot is on each step, if his mother holds his hand or if he holds a railing. Finally, Brian is able to demonstrate walking up the stairs independently holding an animal in each hand while alternating feet (placing only one foot on each step). He may still be holding his arms up and out to the side, a clear sign that he is attempting to find stability and balance during this activity. As his balance improves, he will be able to walk up the stairs with his arms relaxed at his sides or while holding a large, soft toy in front, such as a ball or stuffed animal. Children typically first gain skill and control with ascending versus descending stairs. For instance, a child who is comfortable and safe with walking up stairs by alternating feet may still be placing both feet on each step when walking down steps.

Progression of skill with descending stairs looks similar to the sequence with learning ascending stairs. Brian decides to build a pretend hamburger with his play food. The pieces are in a basket at the top of the stairs, and a plate is at the bottom of the stairs. At first, practice occurs with carrying one item (the bun followed by the meat, lettuce, tomato, cheese, etc.) at a time down the stairs while holding the adult's hand or a railing with the other hand. After practicing for a few weeks, he next is able to carry an item in each hand but continues to put both feet on the same step. If the adult providing assistance notices that he always is stepping down with the same foot first, she may encourage him to let the other foot have a turn to go first sometimes. During this time, Brian may begin alternating feet if he is holding a railing or the adult's hand. Finally, he is able to go down the stairs carrying an item in each hand and still alternating feet. Supervision and adequate guarding from falls should always be used with stair activities. If you notice that the child is holding his arms up and out to the side, instead of relaxing them down near his body, be aware that he is still trying to find stability, and you should be guarding very closely to prevent a fall.

As you practice stair activities with children, you will be working on both ascending and descending stairs, but the activities were described separately to better understand the sequence of progression of these skills.

JUMPING GAMES

Jumping Consecutively

Once a child can jump with a two-foot takeoff and landing (feet moving together), consecutive jumping can be attempted. The goal is to jump like a bunny hopping with both feet moving simultaneously and no stepping between jumps. The child and a sibling or friend can race across the room using this motor pattern. You can set up foam mats on the floor and have her jump from one to the next. If mats are not available, a no-adhesive shelf liner, cut to squares or other desired shapes, works great for this activity because it provides a slip-resistant surface. Before you ask the child to jump, test that the mats do not slide on the floor surface being used. She can pretend to be a frog jumping between lily pads or an adventurer attempting to jump over hot lava or quicksand! Numbering chalk squares can also work well for outdoor play. Create a goal of jumping five, ten, then twenty times consecutively as skill improves.

These squares (or other shapes) can also be used for increasing jumping distance. Place the mats two feet apart and challenge the child to jump from one to the other. Continue to increase the challenge by increasing the distance according to the child's ability. Ideally, you will see her successfully reaching the next mat but putting effort into the jumps.

The mats or chalk squares can also be used to create a hopscotch game that builds consecutive jumping or hopping skill. If the child has not learned to hop on one foot, she can jump with two feet together into the single squares. The pattern and placement of the squares determines the sequence of switching between jumping with feet apart into the double squares and hopping on one foot or jumping with feet together into the single squares.

Jumping Over an Object

Jumping over an object of height is an additional challenge. You can start with a jump rope placed on the ground. You and the child can pretend that the rope is a sleeping snake that you have to jump over without stepping on it and waking it up. If this skill is performed with ease, recruit a reliable helper to assist with holding the rope one to two inches off the ground. Be ready to drop the rope and catch the child if necessary. Increase the height of the rope as the ability of the child improves over time. Ultimately, a good goal may be to jump over a rope at the height of the child's knees, but work up to this level of difficulty gradually, one inch at a time. Always consider safety first and be ready to drop the rope as necessary to prevent the child from tripping and falling if it appears that the height of her jump will not clear the rope. Only perform this skill with trustworthy adults assisting. Siblings and friends may be unpredictable and compromise the safety of the activity.

BALANCE BEAM OR LINE WALKING

Most of us do not have a balance beam in our home but can still practice this skill without buying equipment. Walking on a curb is an excellent way to practice taking steps on a narrow, elevated surface. Hold the child's hand while he attempts to walk on the curb. If he is able to walk steadily without swaying and pulling you or leaning on you, he may want to attempt to try this activity without assistance. However, even if you are not holding his hand, walk in close proximity to the child so that you can catch him if he loses his balance.

You can also draw a balance beam with chalk. A narrower line, two inches wide versus five inches wide, is more challenging. Choose the width that best matches the child's ability. For an additional challenge, have the child try to walk with heels touching toes in tandem steps so that there is no space between his feet. Since you already have set out the chalk, you can place it at one end of the line, and have the child draw a picture at the other end of the line. Each repetition across the line to get a new color for the picture is excellent practice! This activity also can be progressed to walking backward. First try to have the child walk backward on the line without stepping off. If he is able to do this skill with ease, he can try tandem steps with the heel of the front foot touching the toes of the back foot. Some children will attempt all of these methods in one afternoon and some may gradually progress to backward walking over a few weeks or months. Progress depends on age, strength, balance, previous skill level, and experience.

These same line walking activities can easily be moved indoors by using a taped line (masking tape works well) of the width of your selection, according to the skill level of the child. I recommend using a test piece to check that the tape will not damage your chosen floor surface and cannot make any guarantees regarding this potential problem. If you are worried about your floor, it is better to keep the activity outdoors. If you are less concerned and have tried a tape test, indoor line walking can be fun. I do recommend that you do not leave the tape on your carpet or floor beyond your play session time because there will be residue build up over time.

Balance beam and line walking activities provide some of the greatest creative play opportunities. Outdoors, my children like to collect things, such as rocks, flowers, leaves, etc. The collecting basket is placed at one end of the line so that they walk on the line to place their items. A line can serve as a bridge in any game of make-believe, such as taking a doll to a pretend school or taking an imaginary "bad guy" to jail. Many of my patients enjoy playing preschool level board games where they get one turn to pick a card or spin the spinner with each pass across the balance beam. The best games often emerge spontaneously. A number of examples of possible activities to encourage eager participation in this activity were mentioned when sidestepping was discussed. These suggestions included the following:

- Walking across a bridge to attend a tea party

- Placing puzzle pieces with the pieces at one end of the beam or line and the board at the other

- Engaging in a play pirate sword fight after crossing the bridge

- Rescuing people or pets from a pretend fire after carrying a foam cylinder "hose" across the bridge

- Activating a simple light-up switch toy

- Placing rings on a ring stacker

- Placing people or farm animals in a house or barn play set

- Pretending to be an Olympic gymnast

- Building a pretend meal, such as a pizza (one slice at a time) or a sandwich, with play food

- Crossing a bridge to find treasure (gold star stickers)

- Taking a turn at a board game

- Building a train track, one or two pieces at a time, with the pieces at one end of the beam or line and the train table at the other

- Building block towers, houses, or formations

- Dressing a doll at one end of the beam or line by carrying the clothes, one item at a time, from the other end of the beam or line

- Picking one card after each time across the beam or line while playing a card game

Your choice of activity is determined by the cognitive level, ability, and interest of the child. Allow his imagination to take over while you enrich his ideas by combining them with a motor challenge!

OBSTACLE COURSE

Therapists have amazing equipment options for obstacle courses, but parents and teachers can design an obstacle course in their home or classroom to incorporate many of the skills already discussed. Include the activities that you want to practice, depending on the skill level of the children participating. A single course can also be used for more than one child with different strengths and skill sets. The following obstacle course description is an example and may need to be modified to accommodate the ability level of the children participating in the activities. For instance, mats can be placed a greater distance apart for a more advanced jumping challenge, or hopping can be used instead of jumping. A pillow can be placed inside the hula hoop to create more of a balance challenge than standing on a firm, even surface. Line walking can be performed either forward or backward and with tandem steps or without the heel touching the toes.

Set up two toy containers about three feet apart, one hula hoop on the ground, three foam mats or no-adhesive shelf paper squares in a line, and one taped line in sequence across a room. Each child skips, gallops, hops, or jumps consecutively around the containers to complete a figure eight. Next, she jumps or hops into the center of the hula hoop, balances on one foot for a predetermined number of seconds in the center, and jumps or hops over the other side. Then, the child jumps or hops to each mat, with the distance between the mats set according to the ability of the child. Line walking is performed forward or backward, with the heel touching the toes with each step if she is capable of using tandem steps. Finally, the child skips, gallops, hops, or jumps consecutively back to the starting location and waits for her next turn.

GAMES WHILE STANDING ON ONE FOOT

Gaining adequate strength and balance to stand on one

foot for more than a few seconds may take some practice. Since the games discussed here are balance activities, they present a fall risk and demand that you are ready to assist if needed. Being ready to prevent a fall means that you are standing within reach of the child with arms ready to catch him or help him regain balance, not standing across the room. If it is difficult for the child to stand on one foot for more than five seconds, he can try one foot standing with the other foot resting on a stationary and stable object, such as a large block. This activity practices the weight shift of one foot standing while still allowing for some support for balance from the other side. This skill can be progressed to standing with one foot on a soccer or playground ball (a less stable surface) and trying to count to greater than twenty or sing a song while maintaining the position. You may need to hold the ball steady while the child places his foot to start the activity.

Once the child is able to perform independent one foot standing for more than twenty seconds with ease and has proven his stability in this position, he can attempt some additional challenges. For instance, he can play a game of catch while balancing on one foot. The game is more difficult with a smaller or heavier ball so progress as able to challenge, but not frustrate, the child. For example, it is more difficult to maintain balance in single limb stance while catching a playground ball versus a beach ball. Any game that requires upper extremity and trunk movement, such as darts or beanbag toss, can be used to increase both the difficulty and fun of one foot standing. If a child is not interested in these games, he can even try upper extremity dance motions while standing on one foot! Remember to alternate between the right and left legs. These enjoyable games lead us to our next set of gross motor play activities: gross motor challenges using ball skills.

CHAPTER 5

PLAY BALL

Most children love ball play. You don't have to participate in an organized sport to learn fun games to play with balls. In fact, most toddlers and preschoolers do not have the maturity to engage in competitive play but still enjoy learning ball skills.

THROWING

Beginning throws are rolls. Once a child has adequate balance to reach for toys in a sitting position, he can start engaging in ball play. Not only is rolling a start to learning reciprocal play (rolling the ball back and forth with another person such as a parent or sibling), it is a precursor to underhand throwing and some sports and recreational activities. Overhand and underhand throwing are the two basic kinds of throws.

Overhand throwing means that the ball is released with the palm of the throwing arm facing downward or outward and the hand positioned over the ball. Initially, action is achieved more from extending the elbow and flinging the ball forward. In addition to minimal shoulder use, the feet may remain still and little to no rotation of the body is seen. As skill is gained with overhand throwing, a starting position of shoulder abduction, external rotation, and extension is used, which generates more power as the arm moves forward with the shoulder internally rotating and the elbow extending. In other words, the arm begins up, out to the side, and back with the elbow bent and the palm of the hand facing forward. A mature throwing pattern also involves weight shifting forward with a contralateral step (left foot stepping forward if throwing right handed) and body rotation. Beginning a throw by standing sideways to the target, with the throwing arm farther away, encourages more mature throwing mechanics. This pattern includes pivoting on the back foot, shifting weight forward to the leg opposite the throwing arm, and rotating the hips and the trunk to face the target as the throw is executed. Practice may be required to gain accuracy with releasing the ball at the correct moment in time to hit a target.

Underhand throwing simply means that the ball is released with the palm facing upward and under the ball. Rolling a ball is the beginning to learning this motion. As skill is acquired, greater distance and accuracy are achieved by learning to release the ball at the correct height relative to a target. Throwing a small ball with a mature underhand throw involves stepping forward with the leg opposite the throwing arm and rotating the hips and trunk to face the intended target. Movement is generated from the shoulder instead of just flinging the ball forward by bending the elbow. Adding the reciprocal step, body rotation, and greater shoulder involvement creates more power with throwing. There are countless ways to practice these skills without purchasing expensive equipment.

Laundry Toss

Practice throwing to a laundry basket placed on the floor. Socks paired and rolled into balls, beanbags, and small balls (two to four inch diameter) all work well for one hand underhand throwing. The same laundry basket can be used for an easy game of basketball. Start with the child about three feet from the basket and have him throw a medium sized ball (approximately six to ten inch diameter) or stuffed animal to the basket. Gradually increase the distance as skill improves over time. Minimize frustration by selecting a distance that allows the child to experience some success. Two hands are used to throw a ball of this size, but different styles of throwing can be practiced, including tossing with hands under the ball and palms facing upward or pushing the ball out from the chest with palms facing forward.

Hit the Target

Practice overhand and underhand throwing to an elevated target, about the height of the child's shoulder. You can use a laundry basket tipped sideways and placed on a chair or a poster or taped target on the wall. Gradually increase the level of difficulty by starting the throw from a greater distance from the target, but avoid frustrating the child. Choose a distance that allows the child to experience success. If he is involving his shoulder in the throwing mechanics, and not just flinging the ball with his elbow, he can begin to practice stepping forward toward the target with the leg opposite the throwing arm. If he has mastered this pattern, he can try starting the throw from a sideways position (with the throwing arm farther from the target). This position encourages lower extremity pivoting and body rotation to aim at the target. If it is helpful, you can point to the leg opposite the throwing arm (left leg if throwing right handed) and remind the child to step forward on that foot.

Knock Over

Arrange a line or formation of empty milk or juice cartons that have been well washed, plastic bowling pins, or lightweight cardboard blocks. You can set up the objects on the floor or on a low surface (lower than the height of the child's shoulder) so that the intended target is at or below the height of the child's shoulder. Both underhand and overhand throws can be practiced. Choose a challenging, but attainable, distance from the target, which may be three feet for beginning throwers or greater than ten feet for children with more practice and experience. Continue to increase the distance from the target according to the ability of the child, but avoid frustration by not exceeding a distance that allows him to be intermittently successful. Both small balls (approximately two to four inch diameter) and beanbags work well for this game.

Take a Step

This game involves a classic game of throw and catch. Choose a ball to match the ability of the child (more information on ball choice below when catching is discussed). Stand facing the child at close distance. Decide if you are playing with underhand or overhand throwing, and throw the ball back and forth. Each player takes one step backward, away from the other player, each time he successfully catches the ball. See how far apart you can get without dropping the ball! This game can also be played with a beanbag or small, soft toy, such as a stuffed animal.

CATCHING

Understanding the developmental progression of catching enables you to more effectively teach this skill. When first learning to catch a ball, a child will often hold her arms straight out in front and wait for the ball to land in place. It is not uncommon to see a child turn away from the ball or close her eyes as it approaches. As she learns to more actively grab the ball, she will trap it to her chest as opposed to waiting for it to land on her arms, but may still be using her forearms, in addition to her hands, to stabilize the ball against her body. At this point, the elbows may start to relax out of extension and flex to around ninety degrees in preparation for catching the ball. It is difficult to catch a small ball, such as a tennis ball, at this stage of development. However, as she learns to catch with only her hands and to keep her eyes on the ball, success with smaller balls can be achieved. Skill with predicting the trajectory of the ball can also be worked on by not always throwing it directly to the child's waiting hands. In sports, you have to "go after" the ball. It does not just come to you. Do not worry about the exact age to expect this progression. Instead, use this description of how catching develops to challenge the child as you see her master each phase. Overall, this progression will typically be seen during the preschool and early school years.

Basket of Balls

Try to challenge the child in a game of catch by gathering several balls of various sizes and having her catch three in a row with each size, starting with the larger balls to gain confidence. Choose balls that are appropriate for the child's skill level, both in terms of size and weight. For instance, a basketball is likely too hard and heavy for this age group. Encourage the child to think of the size of the ball (small, medium, or large) and position her hands to match the approximate size in preparation for catching it. For example, if her hands are wide apart to start when a small or medium-sized ball is thrown, she may not have time to bring her hands together to successfully catch it. Catching with palms up and scooping the ball to trap it to the body is a beginning style of catching. If the child is only inconsistently catching a six to ten inch diameter (medium-sized) ball despite using this immature catching style, continue to practice and allow her to trap it to her chest as needed. If she exhibits more skill and consistency in catching a medium-sized ball from about five feet, encourage her to attempt to catch using only her hands, not her body, to stabilize the ball. In preparation for catching with this more mature style, she should position her arms so that the palms of her hands are facing each other while elbows are bent. This catching activity can be progressed by throwing and catching from greater distances and using smaller balls. Beanbags and soft toys, such as small stuffed animals, can also be used with this activity.

Name that Favorite Thing

Put a new twist on a game of catch where each of you says a food, color, shape, animal, ice cream flavor, or pizza topping during your turn of play. Select your category before you play, and say a word from the chosen category each time you catch the ball before throwing it to the other player. Other categories can be used as well.

Change Position

Add an additional gross motor challenge in areas of balance and strength by playing catch while in half kneeling or single limb stance (standing on one foot). Attempt this exercise only if the position can be maintained fairly easily without playing catch. A half kneeling position can be described as kneeling with your right foot in front and left knee in line with your body or left foot in front and right knee in line with your body. For optimal strengthening, remember to practice both right and left positions with these exercises.

Bounce and Catch

Attempt a game of bounce and catch. You can start by

alternating bouncing and catching a larger ball, such as a playground ball. The child can bounce the ball back and forth with another person or play in place by herself. The game can be progressed to using a tennis ball, first trying two handed catching, then advancing to one handed catching when able. Try to increase the number of consecutive catches.

KICKING

Kicking a ball requires strength and balance. The balance component comes into play because you are standing on one foot while the other leg kicks the ball and creates motion to throw you off balance. Beginning kicking is poking a ball forward with the foot without first pulling the kicking leg back in extension. As skill is gained, a child learns to generate more force by extending the hip in preparation of swinging the leg to kick the ball. He also learns to approach the ball instead of waiting for the moving ball to come to him. Progression from kicking a stationary ball to kicking a moving ball, and from waiting for the ball to approach to moving forward to meet the ball, is achieved with practice and developmental maturity.

Kick to a Target

For the beginner, try kicking a stationary ball to a target or goal of interest. Kicking to knock over a tower of lightweight blocks or empty juice or milk cartons that have been washed out is a favorite activity. Always keep what motivates the child in mind. If you know that the child prefers reading to loud crashing fun, you can set up a book as a target and read one page every time he accurately kicks the ball to the book. This game works well with any toy of interest. Beginning kickers are not typically using force that would break the book or toy (not appropriate for older children). If the child is already interested in sports activities, he can practice kicking a ball to a more traditional goal between two cones, small trashcans, or boxes. Difficulty with these activities is set by the width of the goal (narrower target is more difficult) and the distance of the child to the goal. He can start kicking from a stationary position or first run and dribble the ball toward the goal for a greater challenge.

Tunnel Kick

Try to kick back and forth with the child where you take turns kicking and using your legs as a tunnel for the goal. This activity can be played by stopping the ball in between each kick (more basic) or while keeping the ball in motion. Difficulty can also be increased by standing farther away from each other.

Soccer Drill

Try dribbling the ball around cones or trashcans arranged in a line. This activity requires the control to use smaller kicks but quick reactions and foot movement. The activity is more difficult with a greater number of cones spaced more closely together. If the child is competitive, you can use a timer to bring out his best effort.

Crab Soccer

Try a game of kick/ soccer while maintaining the crab walk position (described when animal walking was discussed) with a goal at each end of a room. This activity involves walking on hands and feet with the chest and abdomen facing the ceiling. The knees are bent, the elbows are nearly straight, and the bottom is off the ground. The palms of the hands are flat to the floor, not in fists or bearing weight on fingertips alone. Some people call this position the "table top" position where the arms and legs are the legs of the table and the chest and abdomen form the top of the table surface. In order to play crab soccer, the child must be able to maintain the crab position in place and add the challenge of lifting his foot to "walk" or kick the ball. If he maintains the position easily, he can play a game of kick in place where you roll the ball to him and he alternates kicking with the right and left leg. Once he gains the strength and balance to support himself during this activity, he can attempt simultaneously crab walking and kicking the ball toward the goal for a crab soccer game. Crab soccer is not just a kicking game! It is a great strength and coordination challenge where the child is working his entire body, including upper extremities, abdominals, hip extensors, and knee flexors and extensors.

Remember that I did not specify exact age recommendations for these games because every child develops at his own pace. Instead, I have indicated a progression of these activities so that when the child has mastered a level of skill, he can move on to the next challenge. For example, if the child kicks stationary objects with ease, he can move on to ball play. Once he consistently kicks a ball placed in front of him without loss of balance, he can practice with targets or goals to increase accuracy and distance. When he is ready for the next challenge, he can advance to kicking a ball in motion, rolled or kicked to him by an adult or other participant.

CHAPTER 6

ADDITIONAL TIPS AND SUGGESTIONS

PLEASE REMEMBER

These activities are designed to be fun and to make children want to try new challenges. Safety is always the first priority! Do not push a child to do skills that she is not ready to do, and always guard her when introducing new challenges until you see that she has mastered them. Do not force a child to do something that she does not want to try. Instead, motivate her with something that is exciting and interesting to her. This ability not only to get a child active and trying new activities, but also to get her excited and wanting to take on new motor challenges, is the magic that I am confident that you can create for the special child in your life. Her feelings of accomplishment and pride will continue to grow along with her strength, skill, flexibility, and endurance.

POSSIBLE CONCERNS

Parents should keep in mind that children develop at their own rate, and there is not an exact timetable to develop gross motor skills. The age that gross motor skills are acquired depends not only on the child's development, but also on opportunity, practice, and motivation to learn these skills. Therefore, I did not include specific or detailed time lines in this book. However, concerns that arise should be discussed with the child's doctor so that he or she can help sort out if there is a need for further investigation. There is sometimes a medical reason for gross motor delay, and the sooner it is addressed, the better the outcome may be. At this point, I am going to repeat myself to stress a very important point. Parents should consult their pediatrician if they notice that their child presents with significant developmental delay relative to other children the same age, excess stiffness of joints or tightness of muscles, involuntary movement (at rest or when attempting another movement), pain complaints during motor activities, unusual alignment or positioning of body parts, or strong side preferences that are not developmentally appropriate (such as limping when walking or avoiding using one hand). This list provides some examples that should be investigated further but is not meant to be comprehensive or all-inclusive since every child is unique with individual strengths and weaknesses. The child's pediatrician can best address these concerns and make additional medical referrals if he or she feels it is necessary.

MESSAGE FROM THE AUTHOR

I hope that you enjoy tackling these motor challenges with the children in your life and that the tools supplied in this book provide the incentive to get them moving! Over the years, I have had great success in motivating both my patients and children with these activities. By reading this book, you have also gained insight into the development of the fundamental gross motor skills. Whether you are a parent, teacher, or therapist, you will have more success in motivating the children in your life to attempt and practice motor skills if you can link their interests to these activities. I am confident that this book will get you started. Have fun!

ABOUT THE AUTHOR

Dr. Cathy (Schecter) Harcke is a physical therapist, licensed by the Physical Therapy Board of California since 1998, with a career focus of outpatient pediatrics since 1999. Previous employers include Lucile Packard Children's Hospital at Stanford and California Children's Services. Dr. Harcke holds a B.S. in Biology from the University of California, Los Angeles (1995) and a Doctor of Physical Therapy (D.P.T.) degree from the University of Southern California (1998). She currently resides in Los Angeles with her husband, seven year-old daughter, and four year-old son.